D1060733

# Country File
# Spain

## Ian Graham

A⁺

**Smart Apple Media**

First published in 2003 by Franklin Watts
96 Leonard Street, London EC2A 4XD, UK

Franklin Watts Australia
45–51 Huntley Street, Alexandria, NSW 2015

*Country File: Spain* produced for Franklin Watts by Bender
Richardson White, PO Box 266, Uxbridge, UK.

*Editor:* Lionel Bender, *Designer and Page Make-up:* Ben
White, *Picture Researcher:* Cathy Stastny, *Cover Make-up:*
Mike Pilley, Radius, *Production:* Kim Richardson, *Graphics
and Maps:* Stefan Chabluk
Copyright © 2003 Bender Richardson White

*Consultant:* Dr. Terry Jennings, a former geography teacher
and university lecturer. He is now a full-time writer of
children's geography and science books.

Published in the United States by Smart Apple Media
1980 Lookout Drive, North Mankato, Minnesota 56003

Manufactured in China

Library of Congress Cataloging-in-Publication Data

Graham, Ian, 1953–  Spain / Ian Graham.
p. cm. — (Country files)  Includes index.
Contents: Welcome to Spain — The land — The people — Urban
and rural life — Farming and fishing — Resources and industry
— Transportation — Education — Sports and leisure — Daily
life and religion — Arts and media — Government — Place in
the world.
ISBN 1-58340-240-3    1. Spain—Juvenile literature.
[1. Spain.] I. Title. II. Series.
DP17.G735 2003        946—dc21        2003042357

9 8 7 6 5 4 3 2 1

## Picture Credits

Pages 1: PhotoDisc Inc/Emma Lee/Life File. 3: PhotoDisc
Inc/Emma Lee/Life File. 4: James Davis Travel
Photography. 7: PhotoDisc Inc/Emma Lee/Life File. 8:
James Davis Travel Photography. 9: Eye Ubiquitous/
P. Thompson. 10: PhotoDisc Inc/Neil Beer.
11: Lionheart Books. 12: James Davis Travel Photography.
13: Eye Ubiquitous/Mike Feeney. 14: Eye
Ubiquitous/Mike Feeney. 15: James Davis Travel
Photography. 16: Eye Ubiquitous/S. Miller. 18: Eye
Ubiquitous/D. Cumming. 19 Eye Ubiquitous/
D. Cumming. 20: Eye Ubiquitous/Paul Seheult. 21:
Spanish Tourist Office, London. 22 top: Spanish Tourist
Office, London. 22 bottom: Eye Ubiquitous/John Hulme.
24: Eye Ubiquitous/Barry Denyer. 25: Eye
Ubiquitous/Bob Battersby. 27: Lionheart Books. 28–29:
Eye Ubiquitous/Mike Feeney. 30: PhotoDisc Inc/Emma
Lee/Life File. 31:PhotoDisc Inc/Neil Beer.

Cover Photo: James Davis Travel Photography.

## The Author

Ian Graham is a full-time writer and
editor of nonfiction books. He has
written more than 100 books for
children.

# Contents

# Welcome to Spain

The Kingdom of Spain occupies most of the Iberian peninsula at the southwestern corner of Europe. Spain also controls the Canary Islands, the Balearic Islands, and five areas on and off the coast of Morocco. The British colony of Gibraltar occupies a tiny peninsula on Spain's south coast.

Spain is one of the most mountainous countries in Europe. It shares common borders with Portugal, France, the tiny Pyrenean state of Andorra, and Gibraltar. Its cool north coast skirts the Bay of Biscay. Most of its warmer south and east coast lies on the Mediterranean Sea.

Spain has influenced other countries for more than 500 years. It was the first European country to establish an overseas empire, mainly in America. Today, Spain is best known as one of the world's most popular vacation destinations.

## Regionalism

Spain's regions have maintained their distinctive identities and customs despite determined attempts to crush them during the Franco era (1936–75). Since then, the diverse cultures, languages, and customs of the regions have been encouraged and celebrated.

Calle Alcalá in the capital city, Madrid. The streets are lined with stores and offices and filled with pedestrians and traffic. ▼

4

ATLANTIC OCEAN

Bay of Biscay

FRANCE

44°N

Golfe de Gascogne

La Coruña

Gijón

PYRENEES

Golfe du Lion

Santander

Oviedo

Bilbao

San Sebastián

CORDILLERA CANTABRICA

ANDORRA

42°N

Santiago de Compostela

Villablino

Vitoria

Pamplona

Figueres

Gerona

Vigo

Orense

SIERRA CABRERA

León

Logroño

SISTEMA IBERICO

Zaragoza

Ebro

Lérida

Tarrasa

COSTA BRAVA

Esla

Burgos

Barcelona

Valladolid

Duero

Tarragona

Zamora

Salamanca

Segovia

Menorca

40°N

Guadalajara

Mallorca

Palma

S P A I N

MADRID

Tajo

Toledo

MESETA CENTRAL

Valencia

Ibiza

BALEARIC ISLANDS

Cáceres

Trujillo

MONTES DE TOLEDO

Júcar

Alcira

Ibiza

Badajoz

Guadiana

Ciudad Real

Albacete

Alcoy

Formentera

38°N

Puertollano

Alcaráz

SIERRA DE SEGURA

Alicante

PORTUGAL

Nerva

SIERRA MORENA

Linares

Murcia

Guadalquivir

Córdoba

Martos

Lorca

Huelva

Sevilla

Granada

Cerro de Mulhacén

Cartagena

Antequera

SIERRA NEVADA

Almería

MEDITERRANEAN SEA

Jerez de la Frontera

Golfo de Cadiz

Cádiz

Málaga

COSTA DEL SOL

36°N

Marbella

Gibraltar

Strait of Gibraltar

Ceuta

ALGERIA

Melilla

34°N

CANARY ISLANDS

Lanzarote

Arrecife

La Palma

Santa Cruz de La Palma

Tenerife

Fuerteventura

Santa Cruz de Tenerife

Puerto del Rosario

N W E S

Gomera

Teide

Las Palmas

Hierro

Gran Canaria

M O R O C C O

8°W    6°W    4°W    2°W    0°    2°E

Mountains    △ Mountain peak

Grassland and farming

□ Capital    ○ Major city

Country boundary

0    200 Miles

0    200 Kilometers

# The Land

**M**ost of the central part of Spain consists of a great, almost treeless, plateau called the Meseta (meaning Tableland) Central. The Meseta is crossed by the Central Sierras mountain range.

The Meseta Central plateau is framed by a series of mountain ranges. The Cantabrian mountains (Cordillera Cantábrica) lie to the north, the Sierra Morena to the south, and the Iberian Cordillera (Sistema Ibérico) to the east. The Pyrenees stretch 275 miles (440 km) across the neck of the peninsula and separate it from France.

The highest mountain in Spanish territory is Teide Peak on Tenerife, in the Canary Islands. It rises to an altitude of 12,306 feet (3,751 m). On the Spanish mainland, the highest peak is Mulhacén, near the south coast. It rises to 11,420 feet (3,481 m).

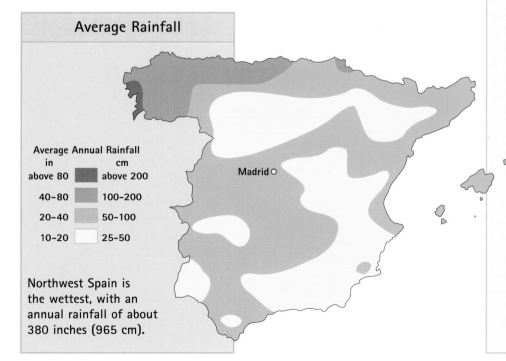

### Average Rainfall

**Average Annual Rainfall**

| in | cm |
|---|---|
| above 80 | above 200 |
| 40–80 | 100–200 |
| 20–40 | 50–100 |
| 10–20 | 25–50 |

Madrid ○

Northwest Spain is the wettest, with an annual rainfall of about 380 inches (965 cm).

## Wildlife

Spain has rich and varied animal and plant life. Its closeness to Africa means that it is home to many African species, including an occasional invasion by desert locusts.

Mammals:
European wolf, brown bear, barbary ape (in Gibraltar), wild boar, ibex, wild goat, red deer, fallow deer, pardel lynx, Egyptian mongoose, blind mole, red squirrel, dormouse, weasel, stone marten, genet, bat, rabbit, hare, fox, and monk seal.

Birds:
Imperial eagle, golden eagle, Bonnelli's eagle, booted eagle, griffon vulture, black vulture, peregrine falcon, marsh harrier, woodpecker, eagle owl, barn owl, buzzard, red kite, black-shouldered kite, white stork, goshawk, azure-winged magpie, golden oriole, and pheasant.

Reptiles and amphibians:
Gecko, fire salamander, marbled newt, ocellated lizard, smooth snake, whip snake, green tree-frog, midwife toad, and chameleon.

Rainfall and snow-melt on Spain's mountains create an extensive river system. Major rivers include the Tagus (Spanish *Tajo*), Ebro, Duero, Guadiana, and Guadalquivir. Of these, only the Ebro drains into the Mediterranean Sea. All the others flow into the Atlantic Ocean.

## Climate

Spain has a varied climate resulting from its size, its mountain ranges, and its closeness to both the Atlantic Ocean and the Sahara Desert. Northern Spain has a temperate and humid climate. The rest of the country has a more Mediterranean climate—cooler and drier inland; hotter and more humid around the coast.

The mountain ranges influence the climate by casting "rain shadows" downwind, creating large arid areas. The Canary Islands, off the coast of northwest Africa, have a summer-like, sub-tropical Atlantic climate all year round. The Balearic Islands, off Spain's east coast, have mild winters and hot, dry summers.

▲ A hilltop village with a backdrop of mountains near the east coast of Spain. Here the summers are hot and the land becomes parched.

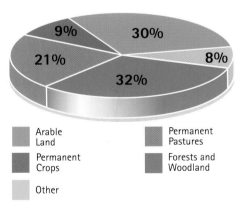

9% 30% 8% 21% 32%

Arable Land
Permanent Pastures
Permanent Crops
Forests and Woodland
Other

▲ Land use in Spain. Less than 10 percent of land is urban, but much of the rest is too hilly or dry to grow crops.

# The People

S pain has a population of approximately 40 million people. They are the descendants of the many peoples who have invaded and settled in Spain throughout recorded history.

Celts, Basques, Phoenicians, Greeks, Carthaginians, Romans, Vandals, Visigoths, and North Africans have all made their home in the Iberian peninsula at different times. Each new wave of settlers fought for land and defended it against new invaders. As a result, Spain became a patchwork of different kingdoms until the Romans brought them under a single political system in the third century B.C. The Visigoths, who invaded the country from Germany in the fifth century, imposed Catholicism on the population. Moors (Muslim Arabs from north Africa) invaded and controlled the country until the end of the 15th century. Marriages between the royal families of the old kingdoms and the defeat of the Moors finally unified the country.

## Language

Most people in Spain speak the country's official language, Castilian. About 75 percent of the population speak it as their first language. The Spanish constitution allows the regions to have their own languages and dialects. In Catalonia, the Balearic Islands, and Navarre, Catalan is spoken. Basque is spoken in the Basque Country, Aragonese in Aragon, and Galician in Galicia.

Other minority languages without official status are protected by law. Most people who speak a regional language also speak Castilian as a second language.

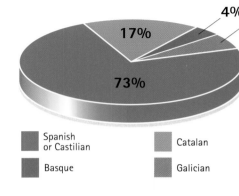

4%

17%

73%

■ Spanish or Castilian     ■ Catalan

■ Basque     ■ Galician

▲ After Castilian, the most widely spoken language in Spain is Catalan, followed by Galician and Basque.

A fruit and vegetable stall in Málaga, where Spaniards speak Castilian. ▼

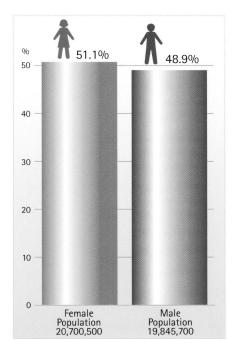

▲ There are significantly more women than men in Spain's population.

▲ Traditional Spanish dancing in a square in Las Palmas, Gran Canaria, one of the Canary Islands.

## Population

Most people live in and around the Madrid area and along the east and south coasts. No region is heavily populated.

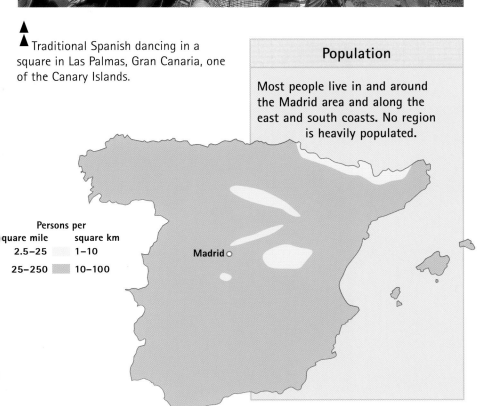

| Persons per | |
| square mile | square km |
| 2.5–25 | 1–10 |
| 25–250 | 10–100 |

Madrid ○

### Web Search ►►

► http://www.ine.es/en/welcome_en.htm
*Web site of the Spanish National Statistics Institute, including a downloadable publication,* Spain in Figures, *with data on Spain's population, transportation, education, etc.*

► http://unstats.un.org/unsd/demographic/social/population.htm
*Population data for countries including Spain, provided by the United Nations (UN) Statistics Division.*

# Urban and Rural Life

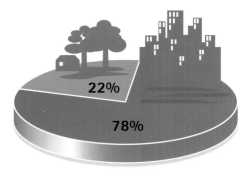

22%

78%

■ Percentage of Population
Living in Urban Areas

■ Percentage of Population
Living in Rural Areas

▲
▲ Three out of every four people live in
towns and cities.

## Back in Time

People first arrived in the
Iberian peninsula 35,000 years
ago. About 5000 B.C., they
were joined by people from
north Africa. Everyone lived in
villages and cultivated the
land. In about 1500 B.C., they
started spreading from the
coast into the interior. In
1100 B.C., Phoenicians from the
area known today as Lebanon
were the first Mediterranean
people to arrive.

These stone houses and a village
church, all with red-tiled roofs, are
near Santillana, close to the northern
coast of Spain. ▶▶

10

**M**ore than three-quarters of the people in Spain
live in towns and cities. Until the 1950s, the
population was largely rural and heavily dependent on
agriculture. Increasing industrialization prompted
people to move from the countryside into the towns
and cities to look for work in the new industries.

This process of urbanization occurred later in Spain than
in the rest of Europe. In 1953, only 53 percent of the
population was urban. By 1980, that had increased to 75
percent. Now, it is more than 78 percent. About 40 percent
of Spain's population live in only 10 cities.

As the nation prospered, people's standard of living rose.
However, living standards and personal income did not rise
uniformly across the whole country. While incomes in the
cities are higher today than the European average, parts of
Andalucia in the south and Extremadura in the west are
among the poorest regions in the European Union (EU).

## Busy cities and quiet villages

Spain's cities are fast-paced, crowded, built-up, noisy, and often congested with traffic. In city centers, the streets are lined with shops and offices. At night, the city streets are still busy as people go out for the evening.

Village life in the countryside is more peaceful and slower. There is less traffic and less of the air pollution that goes with it. The streets are frequently narrow and winding, and the buildings are smaller, more picturesque, and laid out in a less planned way. Goats and sheep are sometimes driven through the streets. Instead of supermarkets, local butchers, grocers, hardware stores, and other small shops thrive.

The country's regions used to be easily distinguished by different styles of dress. Nowadays, suits, casual clothes, or jeans and T-shirts are worn everywhere. Traditional dress is seen only on special occasions such as weddings and fairs.

In most cities, people live in apartment buildings or in houses in the suburbs. These are rented apartments in Madrid.

### Web Search ►►

► http://www.cia.gov/ cia/publications/ factbook/geos/sp.html
*Spain's entry in the CIA World Factbook, with data about the country and its people, government, economy, etc.*

# Farming and Fishing

Agriculture declined in Spain as people moved off of farms into cities and other industries grew, but it is still an extremely important part of the Spanish economy, as is fishing.

One person in twelve works in agriculture. About 42 million acres (17 million ha) of land is cultivated, with 30 million acres (12 million ha) under permanent crops. More than half of the cultivated land lies in only three regions—Andalucia, Castilla y León, and Castilla-La Mancha.

The main crops grown are cereals, especially wheat and barley, and rice. Spanish farming is less industrialized than that in many other west European countries. Family-run farms dominate agriculture. Families account for two-thirds of the total agricultural workforce of 1.2 million.

DATABASE

## Livestock farming

| | |
|---|---|
| Cattle | 6.3 million |
| Sheep | 21.0 million |
| Goats | 2.7 million |
| Pigs | 22.0 million |
| Poultry | 182.0 million |

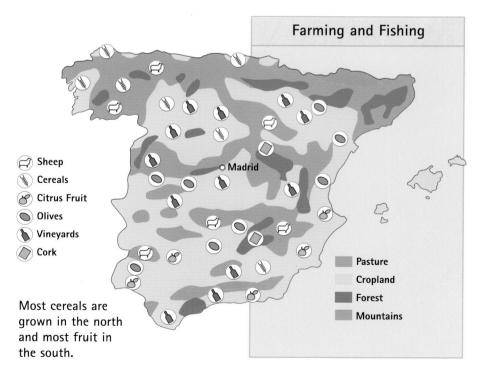

### Farming and Fishing

- Sheep
- Cereals
- Citrus Fruit
- Olives
- Vineyards
- Cork

○ Madrid

Pasture
Cropland
Forest
Mountains

Most cereals are grown in the north and most fruit in the south.

▲ Harvesting melons grown under plastic in Almeria on the southern coast of Spain.

Commercial Fishing

Spain consumes more seafood per person than any other country in the European Union. Its fishing fleet is bigger than all the other fishing fleets of Europe added together. It has 18,900 fishing vessels. Most of them fish in Spanish waters. The main fishing ports are Vigo and La Coruña.

◄◄ A fish auction in Santa Pola, a small town on the east coast.

Web Search ►►

► http://www.fao.org
*The Spain section of the UN Food and Agricultural Organization provides data and statistics on agriculture and farming.*

## Wine and olives

Spain is one of the world's biggest wine producers. About 2.5 million acres (1 million ha) of vineyards produce grapes for the wine industry. The wine most often associated with Spain is Rioja, named after the region where it is made. There are 40 wine-making regions in all. One of them, Jerez de la Frontera, is world-famous for the production of sherry.

More than five million acres (2 million ha) of land are planted with olive groves, mostly for the production of olive oil. The warm climate in the southern part of the country is ideal for growing citrus fruit, especially oranges, and early ripening produce such as tomatoes and avocados for export to northern Europe.

Barley is the main farming crop, followed by wheat and corn.

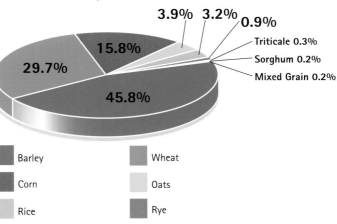

3.9%  3.2%  0.9%
15.8%
29.7%
45.8%

Triticale 0.3%
Sorghum 0.2%
Mixed Grain 0.2%

Barley          Wheat
Corn            Oats
Rice            Rye

# Resources and Industry

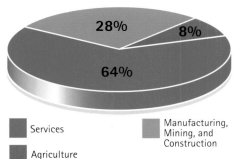

- Services
- Agriculture
- Manufacturing, Mining, and Construction

28%
8%
64%

▲ Proportion of workers in major industries. Service industries increasingly grow while manufacturing declines.

Spain is rich in mineral resources. It has large deposits of sulphur, mercury, nickel, copper, lead, phosphates, and uranium. However, they often lie in folded or faulted rock around the edge of the Meseta Central, making them difficult to mine.

Coal is also an important mined resource. Mines in Asturias and along the Sierra Morena make Spain one of Europe's biggest producers of coal and lignite (a low-quality, woody type of coal). Although Spain has substantial coal deposits, it has very little oil and natural gas resources. Most of its oil and gas needs are met by costly imports. As a result, Spain's economy has traditionally run a large trade deficit.

## Manufacturing and textiles

Spain's leading manufacturing industry is vehicle production. Most of the three million or so vehicles that are made each year are exported, with 90 percent of them going to other EU countries. The country's steel and ship-building industries are facing serious competition from Japan and Korea, where production costs are lower.

The demand for tourist accommodation and a shortage of high-quality housing have produced a strong construction industry. Spain is a major producer and exporter of textiles and clothing. This earns the country more than $22 billion a year and provides employment for one in ten people in the industrial workforce.

◄◄ Quarrying marble for the construction industry. Much of the marble is exported.

# Gross Domestic Product

As in many other developed countries, Spain's economy is dominated by services. In Spain's case, these are mainly tourism, finance and banking, retail, telecommunications, and transportation. Together, they account for about 64 percent of the country's gross domestic product (GDP).

Oil tanker and refinery on the south-east coast. ►►

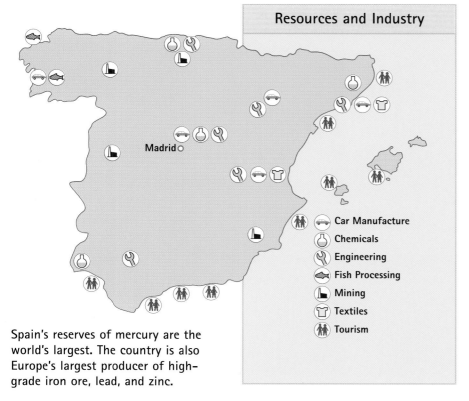

## Resources and Industry

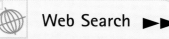

Madrid○

- 🚗 Car Manufacture
- ⚗ Chemicals
- 🔧 Engineering
- 🐟 Fish Processing
- ⬛ Mining
- 👕 Textiles
- 👥 Tourism

Spain's reserves of mercury are the world's largest. The country is also Europe's largest producer of high-grade iron ore, lead, and zinc.

## Web Search ►►

► http://minerals.usgs.gov
*Web site of the U.S. Geological Survey, with information about the mineral reserves and mining output of different countries, including Spain.*

► http://minerals.usgs.gov/ minerals/pubs/country/ 2000/9438000.pdf
*A mineral map of Spain provided by the U.S. Geological Survey.*

► http://unstats.un.org/ unsd/demographic/ social/unempl.htm
*Unemployment statistics for countries including Spain, provided by the United Nations Statistics Division.*

# Transportation

Travel within Spain is generally quick and easy in most places thanks to the extensive road and rail networks and air routes. The main roads and railway lines radiate out from Madrid to all other cities like the spokes of a wheel.

Spain's larger towns and cities are linked by buses and trains. Most rail services are provided by RENFE, the Spanish national railway company. Its *cercanias* (commuter trains) travel within and around major cities. *Regionales* (regional trains) travel between cities. *Largo recorrido* (long-distance) express trains provide long-distance services. Generally, small villages that do not have their own railway stations have bus services.

## Speed Limits

The speed limit on Spain's highways and expressways is 75 miles (120 km) per hour. On other roads, traffic is restricted to either 55 miles (90 km) per hour or 65 miles (100 km) per hour, except in urban areas, where the limit is only 30 miles (50 km) per hour. Tolls are charged on the highways.

A large car and passenger ferry that sails between Spain's east coast and the Balearic Islands. ▼

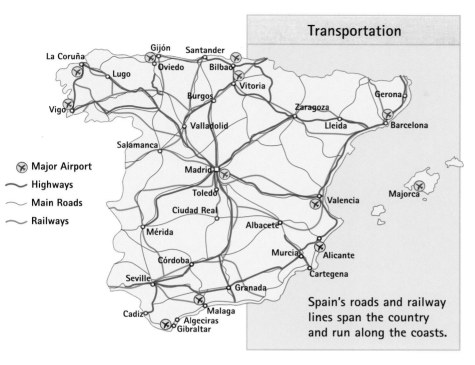

## Transportation

La Coruña · Gijón · Santander · Lugo · Oviedo · Bilbao · Vitoria · Burgos · Vigo · Zaragoza · Valladolid · Lleida · Gerona · Barcelona · Salamanca · Madrid · Toledo · Valencia · Majorca · Ciudad Real · Albacete · Mérida · Murcia · Alicante · Córdoba · Cartegena · Seville · Granada · Cadiz · Malaga · Algeciras · Gibraltar

⊗ Major Airport
∿ Highways
∿ Main Roads
∿ Railways

Spain's roads and railway lines span the country and run along the coasts.

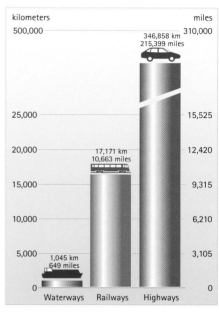

Spain has an extensive and modern transportation network. As well as road, rail, and air, there are navigable rivers and canals for boats and barges.

## Road and rail

In the past, Spain's mountain ranges presented formidable natural barriers to travel over land. The construction of the first railways in the 19th century made it possible for people to travel long distances across the country more easily. Today, more than 500 million long journeys and about 400 million local journeys are made every year by rail. The first highways were built in the 1960s. Today, there are more than 21 million cars on Spain's roads.

## Air and sea

Spain's national airline, Iberia, and a variety of other airlines provide international and domestic air services. More than 40 of Spain's 110 airports handle commercial air traffic. Domestic flights carry 28 million passengers a year. With more than 3,000 miles (5,000 km) of coastline, Spain is heavily dependent on sea travel. It has one of the world's largest merchant fleets. The busiest ports are Bilbao, Algeciras, Tarragona, and Barcelona.

### Web Search ▶▶

▶ http://www.renfe.es
*Web site of the Spanish national rail service.*

▶ http://www.iberia.com
*Web site of Iberia, the Spanish national airline.*

▶ http://www.trasmediterranea.es
*The shipping line that carries passengers between Spain and the Balearic islands.*

# Education

Spain has a literacy rate of about 98 percent, thanks to its free and mandatory state education system. Children enter primary school at the age of six, but they can attend *escuelas de educación infantil* (preschools) before that. Basic primary and secondary (high school) education is free in state schools and mandatory up to the age of 16. Parents can also send their children to private school if they can afford it. About one in three children attend private primary and secondary schools. Children attend school from Monday to Friday.

The school day generally starts at 10:00 A.M. and does not finish until 5:00 P.M. However, there is a long break of about two hours in the middle for the main meal of the day. Private schools and international schools sometimes start and finish their day earlier.

Class in a state primary school in a suburb of Madrid. ▼

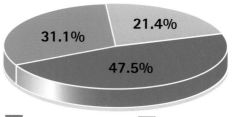

◄◄Children boarding a bus for a school field trip in Barcelona.

21.4%

31.1%

47.5%

| | 6-13 years | | 14-17 years |
| | Higher Education (Universities, etc.) | | |

Students by age range or type of establishment.

## Further education

When students finish their mandatory education, they receive the *Graduado en Educación Secundaria* (certificate of secondary education). This enables them to go on to upper secondary education or vocational training. At the end of this, successful secondary students receive the *Bachiller* diploma. Successful students in vocational training receive the *Técnico* certificate.

The Bachiller diploma entitles students to go on to advanced vocational training or a university. An entrance examination also has to be taken to enter some schools. The Spanish university system is one of the oldest in Europe. Some universities can trace their origins back to the Middle Ages. The oldest, at Salamanca, was founded in 1218. Madrid University dates from 1293.

At schools and universities in regions of Spain with their own language, classes are taught in both the official language, Castilian, and the regional language.

### Foreign Languages

Most Spanish children learn English or French as a foreign language. German is taught in some schools. As part of their language training, and with help from the EU higher education program, many Spanish students spend time at universities in other European countries.

### Web Search ►►

► http://unstats.un.org/unsd/demographic/social/illiteracy.htm
*Literacy statistics for countries including Spain, provided by the UN Statistics Division.*

# Sports and Leisure

The climate in Spain makes golf and tennis popular year-round with residents and tourists alike. Spain's favorite sport is soccer.

National soccer is dominated by two teams—Real Madrid and FC Barcelona. The best teams regularly play in European competitions. Real Madrid has won nine European Championships since the 1950s. Spain's national soccer team reached the quarterfinals of the World Cup in 1998 and 2002.

Hundreds of golf courses have been built around the warm Mediterranean coast. This valuable resource has produced successful home-grown golfers. The best-known, Jose Maria Olazabal, has won tournaments all over Europe, the Middle East, and the U.S.

Sports enthusiasts all over the world turned their attention to Spain in 1992, when 10,500 athletes from 172 countries gathered in Barcelona for the summer Olympic Games.

## Bullfighting

Most towns have a bullring, where crowds gather to watch matadors fight and kill bulls. The spectators enjoy the spectacle of a courageous matador controlling a dangerous animal. It is seen as an art-form. However, many other Europeans condemn bullfighting as cruel.

A matador in action at a bullring in Seville. ▼▼

## Fishing and fiestas

Fishing continues to grow in popularity as a sport and as a leisure activity. Trout, salmon, pike, carp, barbel, tench, and eels can be caught in many of Spain's rivers and lakes. Off the coast, sea anglers catch grey mullet, sea bream, bass, mackerel, and tuna.

Every city, town, and village in Spain has at least one *fiesta*, or festival. Many of them are held on holy days. The most famous fiesta is *San Fermín*, in Pamplona. Its highlight is the *encierro* (running of the bulls), when bulls are released to run through the crowded streets. One of the oddest fiestas is *La Tomatina* in Buñol, near Valencia, when 38,000 people hurl 145 tons (130 t) of tomatoes!

### Pelota

The game of *pelota* (Spanish for ball) or *jai alai* ("merry festival") is particularly popular. Once played mainly in the Basque region in the northeast, it is now played all over Spain and in other parts of the world. Players wear a wicker scoop on one arm to catch the ball and fling it back to another player or against the wall of the pelota court.

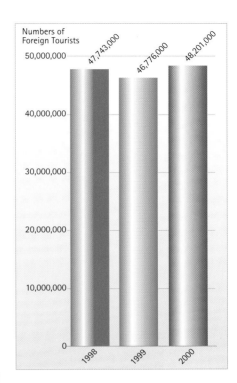

▲ One in every ten tourists traveling outside their own country visits Spain.

A basketball game in the Olympic hall in Barcelona. ▼

### Web Search ►►

► http://www.realmadrid.com
*Web site of the Real Madrid soccer team.*

► http://www.newportgrand.com/histgame.htm
*The history of the game of pelota/jai alai.*

► http://www.red2000.com/spain/toros
*The origins and history of bullfighting.*

21

Festival celebrations in Barcelona.

## Tapas and paella

Eating out in restaurants and bars is very popular. Bars often offer small snacks called *tapas* to eat with a glass of wine or beer. They might be a few slices of cured ham, pieces of fish or octopus, chunks of sausage or cheese, or vegetables. The dish most closely associated with Spain is *paella*, a mix of rice, saffron, meat, and seafood.

*Semana Santa* (Easter Week) procession in Almería on the south coast. ►►

# Daily Life and Religion

**F**ood is an important part of daily life in Spain. At lunchtime, while workers in many countries make do with a hurried sandwich, most businesses in Spain close for at least two hours.

Schools stop for a long lunch, too. This long break for the main meal in the middle of the day is the famous Spanish *siesta*. Because of the siesta, the school day does not end until 5:00 P.M., and the business day does not usually end until about 6:45 P.M. Shops stay open until 8:00 P.M. or even later.

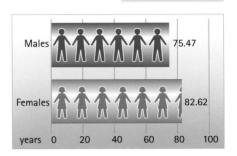

▲ Spanish women live, on average, seven years longer than Spanish men.

## Regional differences
The pattern of daily life is not the same all over Spain. The latest hours are kept in Madrid and the south. Here, for example, the evening meal is not eaten until at least 10:00 P.M., often much later. Northern Spain tends to keep hours similar to the rest of Europe. Many big international corporations based in Spain are trying to adopt the same working hours as other businesses elsewhere in Europe, but few have succeeded.

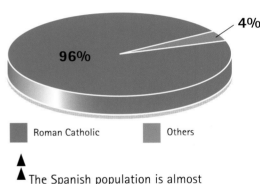

▲ The Spanish population is almost entirely Catholic.

## Religion
Almost all Spanish citizens are Roman Catholic, although most do not attend church regularly. Catholicism was the country's official religion until 1978, when the new constitution broke the link between the state and the church. The constitution protects each citizen's right to religious freedom.

Spain was once a Muslim country, and evidence of its Muslim history can still be seen today. The beautiful Grand Mosque stands in the middle of Córdoba. Parts of it date back to 796 A.D. The magnificent 14th-century Alhambra in Granada was the palace-fortress of Spain's last Moorish rulers.

**Web Search** ►►

► http://www.alhambra-patronato.es
*Web site of the Alhambra, Granada.*

► http://www.idealspain.com/pages/information/culture.htm
*Information about food, drink, fiestas, and traditions in Spain.*

# Arts and Media

Spain is renowned for its great artists and writers. Its rich musical tradition has also produced world-famous musicians, composers, and singers.

Any list of the greatest artists of the last century would include the Spanish painters Pablo Picasso, Salvador Dalí, and Joan Miró. One of Picasso's most famous works, *Guernica*, was inspired by the bombing of the Spanish town of the same name in 1937. The painting now hangs in the Centro de Arte Reina Sofia in Madrid along with other works of modern Spanish art.

Works by great Spanish artists of the past, such as Velázquez and Goya, are displayed in the Museo del Prado, also in Madrid. After the Prado and the Guggenheim Museum in Bilbao, Spain's most visited museum is the Museu Dalí in Figueres. It contains some of Dalí's works and the grave of the artist himself.

## Gaudi

Some of the most dramatic buildings in Spain were designed by Catalan architect Antonio Gaudi (1852–1926). His best-known work is the unfinished temple *Sagrada Familia* (Holy Family) in Barcelona. Gaudi died before the building was finished. Work was restarted in the 1950s and continues today. *Sagrada Familia* is shown on the cover of this book.

## Movies

Early Spanish filmmakers such as Luis Buñuel (1900–83) had to struggle against the repression of the Franco regime to get their films made. Movie censorship ended in 1977. More recently, *The Others* (2001), starring Nicole Kidman, was made by Spanish director Alejandro Amerábar, and Spanish actors Antonio Banderas and Penelope Cruz are major Hollywood stars.

Flamenco dancers in Jerez. ▶▶

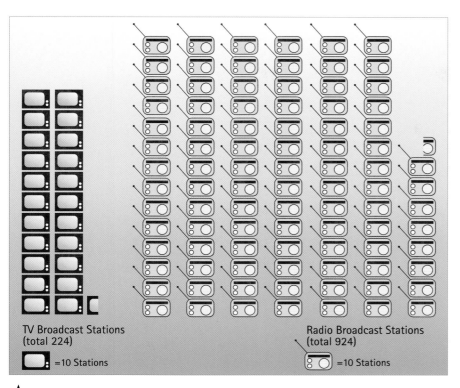

TV Broadcast Stations
(total 224)

Radio Broadcast Stations
(total 924)

☐: =10 Stations

⊚○: =10 Stations

▲
▲ Spain's state television service, TVE, supplies 24 channels. There are many private and local TV and radio stations.

►► A view of the outside of the futuristic metal-clad Guggenheim Museum of Modern Art in Bilbao.

## Music and literature

Music is in the Spanish blood. Flamenco is a passionate style of folk dance and music associated with Andalucian Gypsies. Modern Spain has its own pop and rock bands. Young Spaniards enjoy the same, mainly American, music that is popular throughout the western world. The growing popularity of music with a Latin American flavor has helped to make Spanish artists such as Enrique Iglesias international stars.

Spain also has a long tradition of creative writing. Cervantes' book *Don Quixote*, first published in 1604, describes Don Quixote's adventures with his sidekick Sancho Panza. Spain is still producing writers of international importance. Novelist Camilo José Cela won the world's most prestigious literary prize, the Nobel Prize for Literature, in 1989.

### Web Search ►►

► http://museoprado.mcu.es
*Web site of the Prado Museum, Madrid.*

► http://www.salvador-dali.org
*Web site of the estate of Salvador Dalí, with information about the three museums devoted to his work.*

► http://www.guggenheim-bilbao.es
*Web site with information about the Guggenheim Museum in Bilbao.*

# Government

S pain is a constitutional monarchy. The head of state is a king, but the real power lies with a government elected by the people.

The monarchy and democratic government were both restored in 1978, three years after the death of General Franco. Franco was a dictator who had ruled the country since winning power in a military coup in the 1930s.

Spain is divided into 17 *autonomías* (self-governing communities or regions). These are composed of a total of 50 provinces. At a level of administration below these, there are about 8,000 *municipios* (municipalities), each with its own mayor and council.

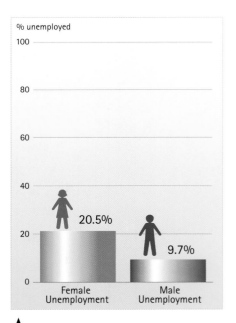

Spain's traditionally high unemployment rate is falling fast because new jobs are being created faster in Spain than anywhere else in the European Union.

Spain's autonomous communities have a high degree of independence from the central government, which is based in the capital, Madrid.

Spain's Regions

Asturias Cantabria Basque Country

Galicia

Navarra

La Rioja

Castilla y León

Catalonia

Aragón

Madrid
Madrid ○

Valencian Region

Extremadura Castilla-La Mancha

Balearic Islands

Murcia

Andalucia

Canary Islands

## Monarchy and the Cortes

The monarch is the head of state, the commander-in-chief of the armed forces, and the symbol of national unity. Since 1975, the monarch has been King Juan Carlos I.

The country is governed by the *Cortes Generales* (Parliament). It is bicameral, meaning that it is composed of two parts, or houses. These are the *Congreso do los Diputados* (Congress of Deputies) and the *Senado* (Senate). The Congress of Deputies is the more powerful of the two. Its 300 to 400 deputies are elected by all citizens over the age of 18. The number of deputies representing each province depends on its population. About four-fifths of the 259 senators are also elected. The rest are appointed by the self-governing communities (*autonomías*). The Cortes is elected for a maximum term of four years.

Until 1999, Spain's unit of currency was the *peseta*. On January 1, 1999, Spain was one of the first European Union countries to agree to give up their own currencies in favor of adopting a new currency, the euro. The transition was completed in January 2002.

▲ Guards stand outside a government ministry building in the center of Madrid.

### Web Search ▶▶

▶ http://www.casareal.es
*Web site of Spain's king and royal family.*

▶ http://www.congreso.es
*Web site of the Congress of Deputies, one of Spain's two legislative bodies.*

▶ http://www.senado.es
*Web site of the Senate, Spain's second legislative body.*

# Place in the World

## Chronology of Historical Events: 300 B.C. to 1600 A.D.

**228 B.C.**
Carthaginians conquer the south and east regions of the Iberian peninsula and make Cartagena their capital

**206 B.C.**
The Roman army defeats the Carthaginians; Spain becomes part of the Roman empire

**415 A.D.**
The Visigoths enter Spain

**711**
Muslim Arabs from north Africa invade Spain and defeat the Visigoths

**756**
Córdoba becomes the capital of Muslim Spain

**1212**
Christian armies defeat Muslim forces

**1233**
Muslim Almohad dynasty collapses

**1469**
Ferdinand II marries Isabella I, uniting the regions of Aragon and Castile

**1492**
The last Muslim stronghold of Granada is captured by Spanish Christians; Catholicism becomes the official state religion

**1521**
Explorer Hernán Cortés conquers Mexico

**1533**
Explorer Francisco Pizarro conquers Peru

**1588**
The Spanish king, Philip II, sends an armada to invade England; it is defeated by England's navy

Spain is a successful modern democracy with a growing economy. It was the fifth-largest economy in the EU in 2001. It is also the 16th-largest exporting country in the world.

Spain was shunned by the international community during the Franco years. Since the end of this repressive era in the 1970s, it has formed closer ties with other countries and joined international organizations. Emigrants returning from abroad brought with them wealth and a desire for the consumer goods they had been accustomed to in other countries. As a result, economic growth in the country was rapid during the 1980s.

Spain maintains close contacts and trading links with many Latin American countries, especially Chile, Argentina, Brazil, and Mexico. It is the single largest foreign investor in Latin America. However, most of its import and export trade is with other EU countries. It is also a member of important international organizations such as NATO (the North Atlantic Treaty Organization), the United Nations, and the European Union.

## International disputes

Spain has a long-running dispute with Morocco over the sovereignty of Spanish territories on and off the Moroccan coast. In 2002, Morocco landed troops on the tiny, uninhabited island of Perejil. Spanish forces ejected them and, in a show of strength, sent warships to protect its coastal towns of Ceuta and Melilla.

## Gibraltar

Spain contests Britain's sovereignty over Gibraltar. Britain captured Gibraltar in 1704, and Spain formally handed it over to Britain in 1713. Spain tried to reclaim Gibraltar in 1963, but in 1967 the colony's 30,000 residents voted to remain British.

Spain closed its border with Gibraltar in 1969. It remained closed for 16 years. In 2002, Britain and Spain discussed sharing sovereignty over Gibraltar, a development that was very unpopular with Gibraltar's residents.

Every year, tourists flock to Spain's beaches, as here near Alicante.

## Columbus

In 1492, the Spanish king and queen financed Italian explorer Christopher Columbus to find a sea route to China and riches by sailing west from Europe. He failed but did discover America.

Spain's imports and exports.

$130 billion
(Machinery, motor vehicles, foodstuffs, consumer goods)

EXPORTS

IMPORTS

$66 billion
(Machinery and equipment, fuels, chemicals, semi-finished goods, foodstuffs, consumer goods)

## Web Search ▶▶

▶ http://news.bbc.co.uk/ 1/hi/world/europe/ 992004.stm

*Part of the extensive BBC News Web site featuring a timeline of modern Spain from the 1930s.*

## Chronology of Historical Events from 1600 A.D.

**1607**
Madrid is made Spain's capital

**1701**
War of Spanish Succession begins when the king dies childless

**1714**
War of Spanish Succession ends with Philip V as king

**1821**
Spain gives independence to Mexico

**1824**
Spanish forces lose in Peru, ending Spanish rule in South America

**1898**
Spanish-American War; Spain loses control of Cuba, Puerto Rico, and the Philippines

**1936–1939**
Military coup and civil war brings General Franco to power

**1975**
Franco dies; King Juan Carlos I crowned

**1977**
First free election in 40 years

**1982**
Spain joins NATO

**1986**
Spain joins the EU

**1992**
Barcelona hosts Summer Olympics

**1996**
Right-wing Popular Party wins general election; Jose Maria Aznar becomes prime minister; he is re-elected in 2000

**2002**
Peseta replaced by euro

**Area:**
194,897 square miles
(504,784 sq km)

**Population size:**
40,546,000

**Capital city:**
Madrid
(Population 5,050,000)

**Other major cities:**
Barcelona (1,635,000)
Valencia (765,000)
Seville (715,000)

**Longest rivers:**
Tagus (Tajo) (626 miles
(1,007 km))
Ebro (566 miles (910 km))
Duero (556 miles (895 km))

**Highest mountain:**
Teide Peak, Tenerife (12,198 feet
(3,718 m))
On Spanish mainland: Mulhacén
(11,421 feet (3,481 m))

**Currency:**
euro
1 euro = 100 euro cents

**Flag:**
Three horizontal bands: red on
top, yellow in the middle, red at
the bottom. The national coat of

arms is on the flagpole side of the
yellow band. The coat of arms
includes the royal seal between the
pillars of Hercules, representing the
two promontories, Gibraltar and
Ceuta, on each side of the eastern
end of the Strait of Gibraltar.

**Languages:**
Castilian (official language),
Catalan, Galician, Euskera (Basque).
Castilian is spoken by most of the
population.

**Major resources:**
Coal, lignite, gypsum, iron ore,
alumina, sulphur, sepiolite, potash,
pumice, feldspar, uranium,
magnesite, zinc, fluorspar,
strontium, barite, lead, peat,
copper, mercury, timber.

**Major exports:**
Machinery, motor vehicles, textiles,
foodstuffs, consumer goods, iron
and steel, petroleum products.

**National holidays and festivals:**
January 1: New Year's Day
January 6: Epiphany
May 1: May Day
July 25: St. James's Day
August 15: Assumption
October 12: National Day
November 1: All Saints' Day
December 6: Constitution Day
December 8: Immaculate
  Conception
December 25: Christmas Day

**Religions:**
Spain is almost entirely Roman
Catholic.

# Glossary

**AGRICULTURE**
Farming the land, including plowing, planting, raising crops, and raising animals.

**ALTITUDE**
The height above sea level of a mountain or an area of land.

**CLIMATE**
The long-term weather in an area.

**CONTINENT**
One of the Earth's largest land masses: Europe, Asia, Australia, North and South America, Africa, and Antarctica.

**COUP**
Short for *coup d'état*, a violent or illegal replacement of a country's government.

**CULTURE**
The beliefs, ideas, knowledge, and customs of a group of people, or the group of people themselves.

**ECONOMY**
A country's finances.

**EMPIRE**
A group of peoples or territories ruled by one country.

**EXPORTS**
Products, resources, or goods sold to other countries.

**GOVERNMENT**
A group of people who manage a country, deciding on laws, raising taxes, and organizing health, education, transportation, and other national systems and services.

**GROSS DOMESTIC PRODUCT**
The value of all goods and services produced by a nation in a year.

**IMPORTS**
Products, resources, or goods brought into the country.

**LITERACY**
The ability to read and write.

**LITERACY RATE**
The percentage of the population who can read and write.

**MANUFACTURING**
Making large numbers of the same things by hand or, more commonly, by machine.

**PENINSULA**
Land projecting into the sea from the mainland so that it is almost an island.

**POPULATION**
All the people who live in a city, country, region, or other area.

**POPULATION DENSITY**
The average number of people living in each square mile or kilometer of a city, country, region, or other area.

**RESOURCES**
Materials that can be used to make goods or electricity, or to generate income for a country or region.

**RURAL**
Having the qualities of the countryside, with a low population density.

**SPANISH ARMADA**
A fleet of warships sent against England in 1588 by Philip II of Spain.

**URBAN**
Having the qualities of a city, with a high population density.

# Index